Bible ESL

Book 2
Lessons 1-5
King Announces Kingdom
Learn English Through the Bible
Harvest Field Publishing
2026

Table of Contents

THE BEATITUDES

Word of the Week = Blessed

MATTHEW 5:3–10

Scan for More

My Lesson Notes

Name: ____

Date: _________________________

My new word: ___________________________________

Notes:

____

____

____

____

____

____

____

____

____

____

This Lesson's Bible Reading

Matthew 5:3–10

Blessed are the poor in spirit, for theirs is the Kingdom of Heaven. Blessed are those who mourn, for they shall be comforted. Blessed are the gentle, for they shall inherit the earth. Blessed are those who hunger and thirst for righteousness, for they shall be filled.

Blessed are the merciful, for they shall obtain mercy. Blessed are the pure in heart, for they shall see God. Blessed are the peacemakers, for they shall be called children of God. Blessed are those who have been persecuted for righteousness' sake, for theirs is the Kingdom of Heaven.

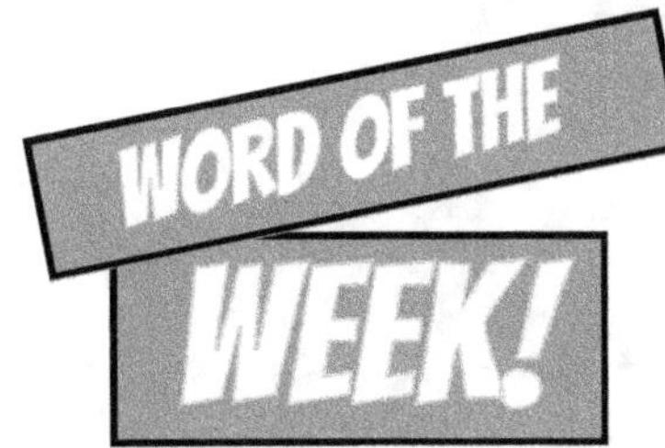

FOLLOW

BIBLICAL DEFINITION

In the Bible, blessed means having God's favor. It does not always mean an easy life. A blessed person trusts God and follows Him. God sees their heart and promises future joy. True blessing comes from knowing God.

Psalm 1:1 — Blessed is the man who doesn't walk in the counsel of the wicked, nor stand on the path of sinners, nor sit in the seat of scoffers.

Matthew 5:3 — Blessed are the poor in spirit, for theirs is the Kingdom of Heaven.

BACKGROUND CONTEXT

Jesus taught the Beatitudes at the beginning of the Sermon on the Mount. Many people believed blessing meant wealth or power. Jesus taught something new. He said God blesses humble people, kind people, and people who want what is right. He said God blesses people who suffer for doing good. Jesus wanted people to understand what God truly values. God looks at the heart, not success.

MODERN DEFINITION

Blessed can mean receiving something good. It can also mean feeling thankful because God is helping you.

SYNONYMS:
Thankful, favored, happy

ANTONYMS:
Cursed, troubled, empty

MODERN-DAY EXAMPLES

1. I feel blessed to have good friends.

2. He felt blessed after finding a new job.

EXERCISE

Try using this word in a sentence and write it below. It can be in a Biblical context or a modern day context.

____

____

____

____

REFLECTION

Jesus teaches that blessing is different from what the world thinks. Many people think success brings blessing. Jesus says blessing comes from a right heart before God. A person can be poor and still be blessed. A person can suffer and still be blessed. God sees faith, kindness, and obedience. Think about what Jesus said. What kind of person does God call blessed? What kind of life do you want to live?

SUPER CHALLENGE

Use the "Word of the Week" at least three times today in a conversation with others. You may write your conversation ideas below.

- ____
- ____
- ____

THE BEATITUDES

✔ WARM UP: *VOCABULARY BUILDING*

Draw a line to match the word to its correct definition.

Humble •	• Kindness to Others
Mercy •	• Doing What is Right
Righteous •	• Not Proud

READING COMPREHENSION

1. Read the passage below and **highlight** or (circle) the vocabulary words given.

After you have finished reading the first time.

2. Read the passage again and underline the words or phrases that are difficult for you.

Jesus taught people on a mountain. He told them who God blesses. God blesses humble people and people who want to do what is right. God blesses kind people and peacemakers. Jesus said God sees them and will reward them.

REFLECT & DISCUSS

Answer the following questions based on the passage read.

What does blessed mean?

____

____

Who does Jesus bless?

____

____

Why does God bless them?

____

____

VOCABULARY CHECK

1. Define these words based on your understanding from the passage:
   a. **Humble** - _______________________________________
   b. **Mercy** - _______________________________________
   c. **Righteous** - _______________________________________
2. Use each of these words in a sentence.
   - _______________________________________
   - _______________________________________
   - _______________________________________
3. Try to find someone you know and explain at least one of these words to them.

QUICK CHECK

Read each question carefully. Circle the letter of the correct answer.

1. Who shows mercy?
      A Kind person   B Mean person   C Proud person

2. What is humble?
      A Proud heart   B Gentle heart   C Angry heart

3. What is righteous?
      A Doing wrong   B Doing right   C Doing nothing

MEMORY VERSE

1. Look for a line from the Gospel story summary.
2. Memorize the chosen line.
3. Practice saying it aloud.
4. Write the verse from memory.
5. Compare it to the original

WRITE & DISCUSS

Write a short paragraph of two to four sentences reflecting on the question below. Write as if you are discussing this with someone close to you. Use the space provided to write down your answer. Use a separate sheet, your journal, or the back of this paper if necessary.

What blessing from God are you thankful for?

____

____

____

____

____

REFLECTION: *Journaling & Sharing*

Reflect on the story you read. Write down your reflection below or in your journal. You can also share them in class, with friends, or with family.

How does this passage make you feel? How can you apply its lessons to your life?

____

____

____

____

____

LET'S DO MORE!

Welcome to the bonus section of our ESL module, where we dive deeper into the world of English language learning! Here, you'll find exciting activities designed to enhance your language skills beyond the core lessons.

GUESS THE WORD

--- Each scrambled word below is related to the passage. Use the provided definitions as clues to unscramble the letters and find the correct word. Write your answer in the space provided.

Example:　**Not known or seen by others** : <u>s e c r e t l y</u> (lyecsetr)

1. Not proud　　　　(H M B U L E)　　＿＿＿＿＿＿＿＿＿＿＿＿＿

2. Kindness to others　(M E R C Y)　　　＿＿＿＿＿＿＿＿＿＿＿＿＿

3. Doing what is right　(R I G H T E O U S) ＿＿＿＿＿＿＿＿＿＿＿＿＿

SPEAK UP: *Try your best if you can!*

1. Find a partner to do this activity with.
2. Write a paragraph or two below or in your journal for someone, reflecting your thoughts and experience.

When do you feel blessed?

＿＿＿＿＿＿＿＿＿＿＿＿＿＿＿＿＿＿＿＿＿＿＿＿＿＿＿＿＿＿＿＿＿＿

＿＿＿＿＿＿＿＿＿＿＿＿＿＿＿＿＿＿＿＿＿＿＿＿＿＿＿＿＿＿＿＿＿＿

＿＿＿＿＿＿＿＿＿＿＿＿＿＿＿＿＿＿＿＿＿＿＿＿＿＿＿＿＿＿＿＿＿＿

＿＿＿＿＿＿＿＿＿＿＿＿＿＿＿＿＿＿＿＿＿＿＿＿＿＿＿＿＿＿＿＿＿＿

BIBLE THREADS

THE CONNECTION BETWEEN THE OLD AND NEW TESTAMENT THAT REVEALS GOD'S PLAN AND PURPOSE

For the exercises below, refer to the original handout as well as the bonus section.

Read and ponder on the Bible passage on the scroll below and answer / do the activities that follow.

Psalm 34:8 — Oh taste and see that Yahweh is good. Blessed is the man who takes refuge in him.

REFLECT & DISCUSS

How can this teaching from the Bible verse or the Bible Threads section help you in your interaction with your family, friends, and community? Write a short paragraph and try to use at least two of the vocabulary words.

____

____

____

____

____

WORD OF THE WEEK

Use the WOW - Word of the Week in a phrase or sentence.

A PRAYER TO GOD

1. Write a short prayer to God, reflecting on the verse above.
2. Write it first in your own language and then in English.

____

____

____

____

____

____

____

ANSWERS:

Reading Comprehension
- Jesus taught about God's blessing.
- God blesses humble and kind people.
- God rewards them.

Quick Check Answers
1 A
2 B
3 B

Guess the Word Answers
1 Humble
2 Mercy
3 Righteous

Scan for More

SALT AND LIGHT

Word of the Week = Light

MATTHEW 5:13–16

Scan for More

My Lesson Notes

Name: ____

Date: _____________________

My new word: _________________________________

Notes:

____

____

____

____

____

____

____

____

____

____

This Lesson's Bible Reading

Matthew 5:13–16

You are the salt of the earth, but if the salt has lost its flavor, with what will it be salted? It is then good for nothing but to be cast out and trodden under the feet of men. You are the light of the world. A city located on a hill can't be hidden. Neither do you light a lamp and put it under a basket, but on a stand; and it shines to all who are in the house. Even so, let your light shine before men, that they may see your good works and glorify your Father who is in heaven.

LIGHT

BIBLICAL DEFINITION

In the Bible, light often means truth and goodness from God. Light shows the right way to live. Jesus said His followers are the light of the world. This means believers should show God's love and truth by how they live.

Psalm 119:105 — Your word is a lamp to my feet, and a light for my path.

Matthew 5:14 — You are the light of the world. A city located on a hill can't be hidden.

BACKGROUND CONTEXT

Jesus taught that His followers should be different from the world. Just as salt changes food, believers should bring goodness to others. Just as light removes darkness, believers should show truth and kindness. Jesus wanted His followers to live in a way that helps others see God. When people see good actions, they can learn about God. Jesus taught that faith should be seen in daily life.

DID YOU KNOW?

MODERN DEFINITION

Light can mean brightness. It can also mean something good that helps people see the right way.

SYNONYMS:
Brightness, hope, guide

ANTONYMS:
Darkness, evil, confusion

MODERN-DAY EXAMPLES

1. Her kindness was a light to everyone.

2. Good teachers bring light to students.

EXERCISE

Try using this word in a sentence and write it below. It can be in a Biblical context or a modern day context.

____

____

____

____

REFLECTION

Jesus said His followers are the light of the world. This means our actions should help others. When we are kind, honest, and helpful, people can see something different in us. Light does not hide. Light shines. Think about your daily life. Do your actions help others? How can you show God's goodness to people around you?

SUPER CHALLENGE

Use the "Word of the Week" at least three times today in a conversation with others. You may write your conversation ideas below.

- ____

- ____

- ____

SALT AND LIGHT

✔ WARM UP: *VOCABULARY BUILDING*

Draw a line to match the word to its correct definition.

Shine •	• helpful actions
Good Works •	• people everywhere
World •	• give light

 READING COMPREHENSION

1. Read the passage below and **highlight** or circle the vocabulary words given.

After you have finished reading the first time.

2. Read the passage again and underline the words or phrases that are difficult for you.

Jesus told His followers they are the light of the world. He said people should see their good actions. These actions help others see God. Jesus wanted His followers to live in a good and honest way.

REFLECT & DISCUSS

Answer the following questions based on the passage read.

What is light?

____

____

Why should we shine?

____

____

How can we help others?

____

____

VOCABULARY CHECK

1. Define these words based on your understanding from the passage:

   a. Shine - _______________________________________

   b. Good Works - _________________________________

   c. World - _______________________________________

2. Use each of these words in a sentence.

   • ____

   • ____

   • ____

3. Try to find someone you know and explain at least one of these words to them.

QUICK CHECK

Read each question carefully. Circle the letter of the correct answer.

1. What does shine mean?

     A. Give light   B. Hide light   C. Break light

2. What are good works?

     A. Bad actions   B. Helpful actions   C. No actions

3. What is the world?

     A. One city   B. One house   C. All people

MEMORY VERSE

1. Look for a line from the Gospel story summary.
2. Memorize the chosen line.
3. Practice saying it aloud.
4. Write the verse from memory.
5. Compare it to the original

WRITE & DISCUSS

Write a short paragraph of two to four sentences reflecting on the question below. Write as if you are discussing this with someone close to you. Use the space provided to write down your answer. Use a separate sheet, your journal, or the back of this paper if necessary.

HOW CAN YOU BE A LIGHT TODAY?

____

____

____

____

____

REFLECTION: _Journaling & Sharing_

Reflect on the story you read. Write down your reflection below or in your journal. You can also share them in class, with friends, or with family.

How does this passage make you feel? How can you apply its lessons to your life?

____

____

____

____

____

 LET'S DO MORE!

Welcome to the bonus section of our ESL module, where we dive deeper into the world of English language learning! Here, you'll find exciting activities designed to enhance your language skills beyond the core lessons.

? GUESS THE WORD

Each scrambled word below is related to the passage. Use the provided definitions as clues to unscramble the letters and find the correct word. Write your answer in the space provided.

Example: **Not known or seen by others** : <u>s e c r e t l y</u> (lyecsetr)

1. Gives light (eihsn)

   o ______________________________

2. Helpful actions (dogo rwkos)

   o ______________________________

3. All people on earth (dlrow)

   o ______________________________

SPEAK UP: *Try your best if you can!*

1. Find a partner to do this activity with.
2. Write a paragraph or two below or in your journal for someone, reflecting your thoughts and experience.

How can you show kindness this week?

____

____

____

____

BIBLE THREADS

THE CONNECTION BETWEEN THE OLD AND NEW TESTAMENT THAT REVEALS GOD'S PLAN AND PURPOSE

For the exercises below, refer to the original handout as well as the bonus section.

Read and ponder on the Bible passage on the scroll below and answer / do the activities that follow.

Isaiah 60:1 — Arise, shine; for your light has come, and Yahweh's glory has risen on you.

⟶ REFLECT & DISCUSS

How can this teaching from the Bible verse or the Bible Threads section help you in your interaction with your family, friends, and community? Write a short paragraph and try to use at least two of the vocabulary words.

____

____

____

____ 

____

WORD OF THE WEEK

Use the WOW - Word of the Week in a phrase or sentence.

A PRAYER TO GOD

1. Write a short prayer to God, reflecting on the verse above.
2. Write it first in your own language and then in English.

____

____

____

____

____

____

____

____

ANSWERS:

Reading Comprehension
Jesus said believers are light.
Good actions show God.
We should live honestly.

Quick Check Answers
1. A
2. B
3. C

Guess the Word Answers
1. Shine
2. Good works
3. World

Scan for More

FULFILLMENT OF THE LAW

Word of the Week = Righteousness

MATTHEW 5:17–20

Bible ESL — Gospel Series
© 2026 Harvest Field Publishing. All rights reserved.

Scripture quotations are from the World English Bible (WEB), a public domain translation.
No permission is required for its use.

No part of this publication may be reproduced, distributed, or transmitted in any form or by any means, including photocopying, recording, or other electronic or mechanical methods, without prior written permission from the publisher, except for brief quotations used in teaching, review, or ministry contexts.

BibleESL.com

Scan for More

My Lesson Notes

Name: ____

Date: ____________________

My new word: _________________________________

Notes:

____

____

____

____

____

____

____

____

____

____

This Lesson's Bible Reading

Matthew 5:17–20

"Don't think that I came to destroy the law or the prophets. I didn't come to destroy, but to fulfill. For most certainly I tell you, until heaven and earth pass away, not even one smallest letter or one tiny pen stroke shall in any way pass away from the law, until all things are accomplished. Whoever therefore breaks one of the least of these commandments and teaches others to do so shall be called least in the Kingdom of Heaven; but whoever does them and teaches them shall be called great in the Kingdom of Heaven. For I tell you that unless your righteousness exceeds that of the scribes and Pharisees, there is no way you will enter into the Kingdom of Heaven."

RIGHTEOUSNESS

BIBLICAL DEFINITION

Righteousness means doing what is right in God's eyes. It means living in a way that pleases God. Jesus taught that true righteousness comes from the heart, not just from rules. God wants people to love Him and live honestly.

Psalm 106:3 — Blessed are those who keep justice. Blessed is one who does what is right at all times.

Matthew 5:20 — Unless your righteousness exceeds that of the scribes and Pharisees, there is no way you will enter the Kingdom of Heaven.

BACKGROUND CONTEXT

Many religious leaders believed following rules made them righteous. Jesus taught that righteousness is more than rules. God cares about the heart. A person may follow rules but still have wrong thoughts. Jesus wanted people to understand that true righteousness comes from loving God and living truthfully. God wants honesty, kindness, and faith. Jesus came to show the true meaning of God's law.

MODERN DEFINITION

Righteousness can mean doing what is right and fair. It can also mean living with honesty and strong values.

SYNONYMS:
Goodness, honesty, fairness

ANTONYMS:
Sin, wrong, evil

MODERN-DAY EXAMPLES

1. He tried to live with honesty and righteousness.

2. Good leaders should act with fairness and righteousness.

EXERCISE

Try using this word in a sentence and write it below. It can be in a Biblical context or a modern day context.

____

____

____

____

REFLECTION

Jesus taught that righteousness starts in the heart. It is not only about rules. It is about loving God and doing what is right even when no one is watching. God sees our thoughts and actions. Think about your life. Do you try to do what is right? How can you show honesty and kindness each day?

SUPER CHALLENGE

Use the "Word of the Week" at least three times today in a conversation with others. You may write your conversation ideas below.

- ____
- ____
- ____

FULFILLMENT OF THE LAW

✓ WARM UP: *VOCABULARY BUILDING*

Draw a line to match the word to its correct definition.

Law   •   • follow rules

Heart   •   • God's rules

Obey   •   • inner life

READING COMPREHENSION

1. Read the passage below and **highlight** or circle the vocabulary words given.

After you have finished reading the first time.

2. Read the passage again and underline the words or phrases that are difficult for you.

Jesus taught that He did not come to remove God's law. He came to show the true meaning. Jesus said people must live with true righteousness. God wants people to obey Him with their hearts.

REFLECT & DISCUSS

Answer the following questions based on the passage read.

What is righteousness?

____

____

What does God see?

____

____

Why should we obey God?

____

____

VOCABULARY CHECK

1. Define these words based on your understanding from the passage:
   a. **Law** - ____
   b. **Heart** - ____
   c. **Obey** - ____
2. Use each of these words in a sentence.
   - ____
   - ____
   - ____
3. Try to find someone you know and explain at least one of these words to them.

QUICK CHECK

Read each question carefully. Circle the letter of the correct answer.

1. What is law?
   A. God's rules   B. Man's ideas   C. Old stories

2. What does heart mean here?
   A. Body part   B. Inner life   C. Food

3. What is obey?
   A. Ignore rules   B. Break rules   C. Follow rules

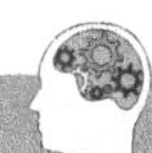

MEMORY VERSE

1. Look for a line from the Gospel story summary.
2. Memorize the chosen line.
3. Practice saying it aloud.
4. Write the verse from memory.
5. Compare it to the original

WRITE & DISCUSS

Write a short paragraph of two to four sentences reflecting on the question below. Write as if you are discussing this with someone close to you. Use the space provided to write down your answer. Use a separate sheet, your journal, or the back of this paper if necessary.

Why is it important to do right?

____

____

____

____

____

REFLECTION: *Journaling & Sharing*

Reflect on the story you read. Write down your reflection below or in your journal. You can also share them in class, with friends, or with family.

How does this passage make you feel? How can you apply its lessons to your life?

____

____

____

____

____

LET'S DO MORE!

Welcome to the bonus section of our ESL module, where we dive deeper into the world of English language learning! Here, you'll find exciting activities designed to enhance your language skills beyond the core lessons.

GUESS THE WORD

Each scrambled word below is related to the passage. Use the provided definitions as clues to unscramble the letters and find the correct word. Write your answer in the space provided.

Example: **Not known or seen by others** : s e c r e t l y (lyecsetr)

1. God's rules (lwa)   : _______________________________

2. Inner life (traeh)   : _______________________________

3. Follow rules (ybeo)   : _______________________________

SPEAK UP: *Try your best if you can!*

1. Find a partner to do this activity with.
2. Write a paragraph or two below or in your journal for someone, reflecting your thoughts and experience.

Why is honesty important?

____

____

____

____

BIBLE THREADS

THE CONNECTION BETWEEN THE OLD AND NEW TESTAMENT THAT REVEALS GOD'S PLAN AND PURPOSE

For the exercises below, refer to the original handout as well as the bonus section.

Read and ponder on the Bible passage on the scroll below and answer / do the activities that follow.

Micah 6:8 — He has shown you, O man, what is good. What does Yahweh require of you, but to act justly, to love mercy, and to walk humbly with your God?

REFLECT & DISCUSS

How can this teaching from the Bible verse or the Bible Threads section help you in your interaction with your family, friends, and community? Write a short paragraph and try to use at least two of the vocabulary words.

____

____

____

_______________________________________ 

____

WORD OF THE WEEK

Use the WOW - Word of the Week in a phrase or sentence.

A PRAYER TO GOD

1. Write a short prayer to God, reflecting on the verse above.
2. Write it first in your own language and then in English.

ANSWERS:

Reading Comprehension
Jesus came to fulfill the law.
God wants true righteousness.
We should obey God from the heart.

Quick Check Answers
1. A
2. B
3. C

Guess the Word Answers
1. Law
2. Heart
3. Obey

Scan for More

BOOK 2

Lesson 4

TRUE WORSHIP AND PRAYER

Word of the Week = Prayer

MATTHEW 6:5–13

Scan for More

My Lesson Notes

Name: ____

Date: _____________________

My new word: _______________________________

Notes:

____

____

____

____

____

____

____

____

____

____

____

This Lesson's Bible Reading

Matthew 6:9–13

Pray like this: Our Father in heaven, may your name be kept holy. Let your Kingdom come. Let your will be done on earth as it is in heaven. Give us today our daily bread. Forgive us our debts, as we also forgive our debtors. Bring us not into temptation, but deliver us from the evil one. For yours is the Kingdom, the power, and the glory forever. Amen.

PRAYER

BIBLICAL DEFINITION

Prayer is talking to God. It is how we thank Him, ask for help, and share our needs. Jesus taught His followers how to pray. Prayer shows trust in God. God listens when people pray with honest hearts.

Psalm 145:18 — Yahweh is near to all those who call on him, to all who call on him in truth.

Matthew 6:6 — When you pray, enter into your room, and having shut your door, pray to your Father who is in secret.

BACKGROUND CONTEXT

Jesus saw many people praying to be seen by others. They wanted attention. Jesus taught that prayer should be honest and private. God cares about sincere hearts. Jesus gave an example prayer to show what matters. Prayer should include worship, asking for needs, forgiveness, and trust. Jesus wanted His followers to pray simply and honestly.

MODERN DEFINITION

Prayer can mean talking to God or asking God for help. It can also mean quietly thinking about God.

SYNONYMS:
Request, talk, worship

ANTONYMS:
Silence, doubt, ignore

MODERN-DAY EXAMPLES

1. She prayed before her test.

2. He said a prayer before dinner.

EXERCISE

Try using this word in a sentence and write it below. It can be in a Biblical context or a modern day context.

____

____

____

____

REFLECTION

Jesus taught that prayer should be honest and simple. God does not want long or fancy words. He wants real hearts. Prayer helps people trust God. Think about your life. Do you talk to God? What would you like to say to Him today?

SUPER CHALLENGE

Use the "Word of the Week" at least three times today in a conversation with others. You may write your conversation ideas below.

- ____
- ____
- ____

TRUE WORSHIP AND PRAYER

✓ WARM UP: *VOCABULARY BUILDING*

Draw a line to match the word to its correct definition.

Prayer •   • To pardon someone

Forgive •   • Talking to God

Temptation •   • A test to do wrong

 ## READING COMPREHENSION

1. Read the passage below and **highlight** or circle the vocabulary words given.

After you have finished reading the first time.

2. Read the passage again and underline the words or phrases that are difficult for you.

Jesus taught His followers how to pray. He said prayer should be simple and honest. God knows what people need. Jesus showed them how to trust God in prayer.

REFLECT & DISCUSS

Answer the following questions based on the passage read.

1. What is prayer?

____

____

2. Why do people pray?

____

____

3. What did Jesus teach?

____

____

VOCABULARY CHECK

1. Define these words based on your understanding from the passage:

   a. Prayer - ____

   b. Forgive - ____

   c. Temptation - ____

2. Use each of these words in a sentence.

   - ____
   - ____
   - ____

3. Try to find someone you know and explain at least one of these words to them.

QUICK CHECK

Read each question carefully. Circle the letter of the correct answer.

1. What is prayer?

   A. Talking to God   B. Talking to people   C. Talking to self

2. What is forgive?

   A. Hold anger   B. Pardon someone   C. Ignore someone

3. What is temptation?

   A. Doing good   B. A test to do right   C. A test to do wrong

MEMORY VERSE

1. Look for a line from the Gospel story summary.
2. Memorize the chosen line.
3. Practice saying it aloud.
4. Write the verse from memory.
5. Compare it to the original

WRITE & DISCUSS

Write a short paragraph of two to four sentences reflecting on the question below. Write as if you are discussing this with someone close to you. Use the space provided to write down your answer. Use a separate sheet, your journal, or the back of this paper if necessary.

Why is prayer important?

____

____

____

____

____

REFLECTION: *Journaling & Sharing*

Reflect on the story you read. Write down your reflection below or in your journal. You can also share them in class, with friends, or with family.

How does this passage make you feel? How can you apply its lessons to your life?

____

____

____

____

____

LET'S DO MORE!

Welcome to the bonus section of our ESL module, where we dive deeper into the world of English language learning! Here, you'll find exciting activities designed to enhance your language skills beyond the core lessons.

GUESS THE WORD

Each scrambled word below is related to the passage. Use the provided definitions as clues to unscramble the letters and find the correct word. Write your answer in the space provided.

Example: **Not known or seen by others** : s e c r e t l y (lyecsetr)

1. Talking to God (reyarp)　　　: _______________________________

2. To pardon someone (gofrive) : _______________________________

3. A test to do wrong (tatimptone) : _______________________________

SPEAK UP: *Try your best if you can!*

1. Find a partner to do this activity with.
2. Write a paragraph or two below or in your journal for someone, reflecting your thoughts and experience.

When do you pray?

____

____

____

____

BIBLE THREADS

THE CONNECTION BETWEEN THE OLD AND NEW TESTAMENT THAT REVEALS GOD'S PLAN AND PURPOSE

For the exercises below, refer to the original handout as well as the bonus section.

Read and ponder on the Bible passage on the scroll below and answer / do the activities that follow.

Jeremiah 29:12 — You shall call on me, and you shall go and pray to me, and I will listen to you.

⤵ REFLECT & DISCUSS

How can this teaching from the Bible verse or the Bible Threads section help you in your interaction with your family, friends, and community? Write a short paragraph and try to use at least two of the vocabulary words.

____

____

____

____

____

WORD OF THE WEEK

Use the WOW - Word of the Week in a phrase or sentence.

A PRAYER TO GOD

1. Write a short prayer to God, reflecting on the verse above.
2. Write it first in your own language and then in English.

____

____

____

____

____

____

____

ANSWERS:

Reading Comprehension
Jesus taught simple prayer.
God listens to prayer.
We should trust God.

Quick Check
1. A
2. B
3. C

Guess the Word
1. Prayer
2. Forgive
3. Temptation

Scan for More

TRUSTING GOD

Word of the Week = Treasure

MATTHEW 6:19–21

Bible ESL — Gospel Series
© 2026 Harvest Field Publishing. All rights reserved.

Scripture quotations are from the World English Bible (WEB), a public domain translation.
No permission is required for its use.

No part of this publication may be reproduced, distributed, or transmitted in any form or by any means, including photocopying, recording, or other electronic or mechanical methods, without prior written permission from the publisher, except for brief quotations used in teaching, review, or ministry contexts.

BibleESL.com

Scan for More

My Lesson Notes

Name: ____

Date: _____________________

My new word: _______________________________

Notes:

____

____

____

____

____

____

____

____

____

____

This Lesson's Bible Reading

Matthew 6:19–21

Do not store up treasures for yourselves on the earth, where moth and rust destroy, and where thieves break in and steal. But store up for yourselves treasures in heaven, where neither moth nor rust destroys, and where thieves do not break in and steal. For where your treasure is, there your heart will be also.

TREASURE

BIBLICAL DEFINITION

Treasure means something very valuable. In the Bible, treasure can mean what a person loves most. Jesus taught that people should value God more than money. True treasure is found in heaven. When people trust God, they choose what lasts forever instead of what passes away.

Matthew 6:33 — But seek first God's Kingdom and his righteousness; and all these things will be given to you as well.

Proverbs 2:4–5 — If you seek wisdom like silver and search for her like hidden treasures, then you will understand the fear of Yahweh.

BACKGROUND CONTEXT

Jesus taught people not to focus only on money and things. Many people worried about what they owned. Jesus said these things do not last. He wanted people to trust God instead. God knows what people need. Jesus taught that people should care more about heaven than earth. What people love most shows what is in their hearts.

MODERN DEFINITION

Treasure can mean something very valuable. It can also mean something a person cares about deeply.

SYNONYMS:
Value, riches, prize

ANTONYMS:
Trash, loss, waste

MODERN-DAY EXAMPLES

1. Family is her greatest treasure.

2. He keeps the photo as a treasure.

EXERCISE

Try using this word in a sentence and write it below. It can be in a Biblical context or a modern day context.

____

____

____

____

REFLECTION

Jesus taught that what we love shows what is in our hearts. If we love money most, our hearts will follow money. If we love God most, our hearts will follow God. Trusting God means believing He will care for us. Think about what is most important to you. What do you treasure most?

SUPER CHALLENGE

Use the "Word of the Week" at least three times today in a conversation with others. You may write your conversation ideas below.

- ____

- ____

- ____

TRUSTING GOD

✓ WARM UP: *VOCABULARY BUILDING*

Draw a line to match the word to its correct definition.

Treasure　　•　　　　　• Believe someone will help you

Heaven　　•　　　　　• Something very valuable

Trust　　•　　　　　• A place with God

📖 READING COMPREHENSION

1. Read the passage below and **highlight** or (circle) the vocabulary words given.

After you have finished reading the first time.

2. Read the passage again and underline the words or phrases that are difficult for you.

Jesus taught about true treasure. He said people should not trust money. Earthly things do not last forever. God's kingdom lasts forever. Jesus taught people to trust God instead of worrying about things.

REFLECT & DISCUSS

Answer the following questions based on the passage read.

1. What is treasure?

____

____

2. Why should we trust God?

____

____

3. What lasts forever?

____

____

VOCABULARY CHECK

1. Define these words based on your understanding from the passage:

   a. Treasure - ____

   b. Heaven - ____

   c. Trust - ____

2. Use each of these words in a sentence.

   - ____
   - ____
   - ____

3. Try to find someone you know and explain at least one of these words to them.

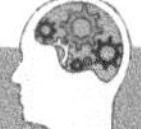

QUICK CHECK

Read each question carefully. Circle the letter of the correct answer.

1. What is treasure?

   A. Something valuable   B. Something broken   C. Something lost

2. What is heaven?

   A. A city   B. God's place   C. A country

3. What is trust?

   A. Fear someone   B. Believe someone   C. Ignore someone

MEMORY VERSE

1. Look for a line from the Gospel story summary.
2. Memorize the chosen line.
3. Practice saying it aloud.
4. Write the verse from memory.
5. Compare it to the original

WRITE & DISCUSS

Write a short paragraph of two to four sentences reflecting on the question below. Write as if you are discussing this with someone close to you. Use the space provided to write down your answer. Use a separate sheet, your journal, or the back of this paper if necessary.

What do you treasure most?

REFLECTION: *Journaling & Sharing*

Reflect on the story you read. Write down your reflection below or in your journal. You can also share them in class, with friends, or with family.

How does this passage make you feel? How can you apply its lessons to your life?

 LET'S DO MORE!

Welcome to the bonus section of our ESL module, where we dive deeper into the world of English language learning! Here, you'll find exciting activities designed to enhance your language skills beyond the core lessons.

GUESS THE WORD

Each scrambled word below is related to the passage. Use the provided definitions as clues to unscramble the letters and find the correct word. Write your answer in the space provided.

Example: **Not known or seen by others** : s e c r e t l y (lyecsetr)

1. Something very valuable (ruseaert) : ______________________________

2. God's home (nehave) : ______________________________

3. Believe someone (rtuts) : ______________________________

📢 SPEAK UP: *Try your best if you can!*

1. Find a partner to do this activity with.
2. Write a paragraph or two below or in your journal for someone, reflecting your thoughts and experience.

Why can we trust God?

____

____

____

____

BIBLE THREADS

THE CONNECTION BETWEEN THE OLD AND NEW TESTAMENT THAT REVEALS GOD'S PLAN AND PURPOSE

For the exercises below, refer to the original handout as well as the bonus section.

Read and ponder on the Bible passage on the scroll below and answer / do the activities that follow.

Psalm 20:7 — Some trust in chariots, and some in horses, but we trust in the name of Yahweh our God.

REFLECT & DISCUSS

How can this teaching from the Bible verse or the Bible Threads section help you in your interaction with your family, friends, and community? Write a short paragraph and try to use at least two of the vocabulary words.

____

____

____

____

____

WORD OF THE WEEK

Use the WOW - Word of the Week in a phrase or sentence.

A PRAYER TO GOD

1. Write a short prayer to God, reflecting on the verse above.
2. Write it first in your own language and then in English.

ANSWERS:

Reading Comprehension
Jesus taught about true treasure.
God's kingdom lasts forever.
We should trust God.

Quick Check Answers
1. A
2. B
3. B

Guess the Word Answers
1. Treasure
2. Heaven
3. Trust

Scan for More

About the Author

Christopher Smith is the creator of Bible ESL, a structured English learning system built around clear, accurate Bible texts. He has years of experience teaching, writing, and developing practical learning tools designed to help students grow in both language skill and confidence.

Bible ESL was created to make English accessible through meaningful content. Each lesson focuses on clarity, structure, and steady progress, helping learners improve vocabulary, comprehension, and communication skills step by step.

Christopher develops all materials with a focus on simplicity, accuracy, and real-world usability.

May God bless you as you continue to grow in your understanding, your faith, and your confidence in English. May His Word guide your learning and strengthen you each day.

Learn more and continue studying:
BibleESL.com
YouTube: YouTube.com/@BibleESL
Instagram: Instagram.com/Bible_ESL
Facebook: Facebook.com/BibleESL